God
Is Calling You

31- Day Devotional
to Help You Pursue
God's Purpose
For Your Life

Faith Wells

WESTBOW
PRESS®
A DIVISION OF THOMAS NELSON
& ZONDERVAN

WestBow Press books may be ordered through booksellers or by contacting:

WestBow Press
A Division of Thomas Nelson & Zondervan
1663 Liberty Drive
Bloomington, IN 47403
www.westbowpress.com
844-714-3454

Scripture quotations marked "King James Version" are taken from the King James Version.

Scripture quotations marked "New International Version" are taken from The Holy Bible, New International Version®, NIV® Copyright © 1973, 1978, 1984, 2011 by Biblica, Inc.® Used by permission. All rights reserved worldwide.

ISBN: 978-1-6642-7470-9 (sc)
ISBN: 978-1-6642-7471-6 (hc)
ISBN: 978-1-6642-7469-3 (e)

Library of Congress Control Number: 2022914414

Print information available on the last page.

WestBow Press rev. date: 10/05/2022

To my sister, my inspiration, Hope Anna Wells.
Thank you for seeing God's gift in me before I saw
it in myself. You are forever in my heart.

Prologue

My prayer:

Lord, let this enter the hands of those who are frustrated, who feel like giving up. Let this enter the hands of those who have fallen away or those who desperately need a relationship with You, God.

Let this enter the hands of those who have experienced hurt after hurt, betrayal after betrayal, and need You to speak to them and give them a clear sign that this is not the end. Let this enter the hands of those who have cried tears of sadness, anger, doubt, and shame, night after night, hoping to just hear Your voice and hoping for You to do something miraculous in their lives.

Let this enter the hands of those who feel tired, confused, abandoned, and misused. Let this enter the hands of those whose minds feel plagued with endless questions concerning Your will and direction for their lives.

Let this enter the hands of the brokenhearted—the ones who've been deceived, abused, and mistreated when all they gave was pure love. Let this enter the hands of those who feel less than and are looked down upon.

Let this enter the hands of those who feel themselves getting weary from the waiting. Let this enter the hands of those carrying just a few drops of hope left.

Let this enter the hands of those carrying the weight of bitterness and anger; those who just can't seem to let go of the past.

Let this enter the hands of those who want to forget the hurt, but all they can do is remember.

Let this enter the hands of those who need to be set free from the burden of unforgiveness. Let this enter the hands of those who are running from You; fearful to live in the purpose You've created them for.

Let this enter the hands of those who need change, the dreamers who desire for You to move and do something new in their lives. Let this enter the hand of those who are desperately calling out to You to turn things around for their favor, for their good, and for Your glory.

Let this enter the hands of those who've been attacked and persecuted. Let this enter the hands of those who trust Your promises, but everything seems so blurry because they can't seem to hear Your voice to give them direction and guidance.

Let this enter the hands of those who need Your help because they can't seem to figure out their lives on their own. Let this enter the hands of those who've felt lonely, insecure, and insignificant.

Let this enter the hands of those who have fought to keep their head held high, looking up to You, the source of their strength and help. Let this enter the hands of those who need signs, miracles, and wonders to take place in their lives.

Let this enter the hands of those who need You to change their lives, transforming them from the inside out. Let this enter the hands of those who have wrestled like Jacob because they know on the other side of their test is a testimony.

Let this enter the hands of those who believe You can turn their mess into a miracle. Let their hope not run dry. Let their faith not be shaken. Let their tears not be wasted. Let their struggle not be in vain, Lord. Use their story for Your glory.

Preface

My love of writing began during my preteen years. From an early age, I've always dreamed of becoming an author. As I grew older, the thought to pursue this passion wafted in and out of my mind. I constantly pondered in my mind whether I was made for this calling. I had no idea where to begin.

Then tragedy struck. In 2018, my younger sister, Hope Anna Wells, was diagnosed with cancer. In 2020, more trials shoved their way into my life, and I began to deal with heavy grief after losing Hope to cancer.

In the fall of 2021, I gave up trying to fix the broken pieces of my life. I began to seek God like never before and decided to completely surrender my dreams, desires, and heart to Him—and that's when God made His presence known in my life. He began to speak to me and assure me that He had never left my side. He spoke promises over my life and assured me of the great plans He had in store for me.

And after asking, begging, crying, seeking, and knocking on His door, He turned the knob, opened the door, called me into my purpose, and gave me the keys to create this God-inspired book, *God Is Calling You.*

I hope that when you digest the wisdom and knowledge off the pages of this book, it is as if God is speaking to you, confirming to you what He has already spoken. I hope that as you read this book, God answers the prayers you pray in this book, and comforts you wherever you may be in life.

I hope that this experience helps you to recognize the voice of God and understand who He is. I hope you discover God in a completely different, incredible, and life-transforming way. It is my desire that this journey draws you closer to God and confirms God's will and calling for your life.

Acknowledgments

I would like to thank Westbow Press for taking on this special project. Special thanks to Michael and Patricia Wells for their encouragement and advice throughout this journey. Thank you, Charity, Hope, Joy, Grace, and Glory for your willingness to walk step-by-step with me throughout my faith journey and for your endless love and support. And most importantly, thank You, Holy Spirit, for Your unending favor, guidance, and wisdom that has helped me create this work of art.

To all the readers who have chosen to take this incredible journey with me, thank you. I hope that this book touches your heart and transforms your life for the glory of God. You are in for a ride.

DAY 1

God Is Calling You

The Lord came and stood there, calling as at the other times, "Samuel! Samuel!" Then Samuel said, "Speak, for your servant is listening."

—1 Samuel 3:10 (New International Version)

March 14, 2022, marks the day the Lord gave me the title for this book, *God Is Calling You*. On that day, God showed me what it looks like when God calls His children. In Samuel 3, we hear about Samuel, who was called by God at an early age. In this passage, when God called Samuel three times, he immediately thought it was Eli, his mentor, calling him and went to him each time he heard the call. Finally, Eli realized that Samuel was hearing from God and told him how to respond to the call if he heard it again. When God called Samuel the fourth time, Samuel responded as Eli directed, "Speak, for your servant is listening."

At that moment, God revealed to Samuel that He was doing something new in Israel, and Samuel was given his first assignment as God's prophet to deliver a timely message. But this was only the beginning of Samuel's ministry. Samuel's ministry continued to grow in great spiritual authority and power. His reliance on God and obedient spirit enabled everything he prophesied to be fulfilled. Throughout his life, God consistently revealed Himself to Samuel, and Samuel brought forth God's Word to the people.

When God calls you, you must respond. Many times, the call from God is for the calling He has for you. Not only must you answer the call, just as Samuel did, but you should also obey the initial assignment He gives you. Your obedience will allow God to continue to work in your life, just as He did in Samuel's life. God's call to Samuel changed the trajectory of Samuel's life, and from that day forward, Samuel began his ministry, prophesying messages from God to the people.

God's call for your life can also change the trajectory of your life. And His call means there is a great divine plan and purpose God has for your life; a plan that is much bigger than you and greater than what you could have ever imagined.

> *And His call means there is a great divine plan and purpose God has for your life; a plan that is much bigger than you and greater than what you could have ever imagined.*

But this cannot be accomplished without the power of the Holy Spirit. The Holy Spirit will give you the tools and direction that are necessary for you to accomplish the task at hand. Rely on Him to lead and guide you into your purpose, and watch God powerfully move in your life. God's call does not compare to anything this world has to offer. His call takes you further. His call takes you deeper. His call takes you higher.

Prayer: "Lord, I thank You for calling me. I thank You for forming my purpose and calling for my life, even before You formed me in my mother's womb. I pray for Your guidance and direction as I walk in the calling You have for my life. I pray You will never cease to speak to me and show me Your plans for my life. Direct me. Guide me. Lead me. Bless me. Make me all that You desire for me to be. Speak to me, Lord, for Thy servant is listening."

Reflection:

- After reading today's devotional, what is one thing that God is saying to you?

- What does 1 Samuel 3:10 mean to you?

- Has God ever called you (spoken to you)? What did He say? What is God saying to you in this season of your life?

- Write down any other thoughts you have.

- Meditate on 1 Samuel 3:10 today.

DAY 2

The Call

As a prisoner for the Lord, then, I urge you to live a life worthy of the calling you have received.

—Ephesians 4:1 (New International Version)

Have you ever sensed God calling you? Have you ever felt as if you were created for a specific reason? Do you crave to know your reason for being? If you've answered yes to any of these questions, I wrote this devotional for you. Before we were even formed in our mothers' wombs, God placed a calling on our lives. God placed you on this earth with a calling, a purpose, and divine destiny. Your calling is like no one else's; it is a unique and customized purpose that God placed upon you.

One thing to note about your calling is that you will feel ill-equipped for it, just like many people from the scripture did such as Moses, Elijah, and Esther. When you receive a call from God, you'll hesitate and question whether you are a good fit for the assignment, but if you trust God, He will fill in the gaps and replace every weakness you sense inside of you with His strength. God always uses the unlikely, the ordinary, the unschooled, the insecure, the misunderstood, the outcast, and the rejected human beings. But

God always promises to empower those He calls. It is up to us whether we receive this promise and move forward in obedience to what He has called us to do.

Calling is about your faithfulness to God today. We must strive daily to be faithful to what God has placed in our lives now and get ready for the unexpected things He will later place in our paths to empower us and guide us where He desires us to be. God normally doesn't show a person the whole path to his or her life's journey. Instead, He shows our path step by step, as we walk in obedience to Him.

Abraham's life shows us that God may tell us to go, without us knowing where exactly He is taking us. God may show us the first step, the next step, and then the next step, and this process continues until we reach our destination. So be faithful and walk in God's path for your life as God orders each step of your journey.

And as he orders each step, you can be comforted by the fact that God will empower you with the Holy Spirit for any task at hand. You will experience a filling of His Spirit that will enable you to powerfully complete the assignments that lie in front of you. Without the Holy Spirit, there is no way anyone can successfully fulfill God's calling.

Without the Holy Spirit, there is no way anyone can successfully fulfill God's calling.

And remember, the Holy Spirit will never cease to assure you of His presence as you daily seek His guidance. God will send confirmation after confirmation in diverse ways as you seek Him. Trust His voice and walk in faith as you obey the calling God has for your life.

Prayer: "Lord, I believe You have a purpose for my life. I believe You have a divine calling You've created just for me so I can arrive at the intended destination You have for me. Lord, tug at my heart so that I hear Your voice and receive the confirmation I need to follow Your call for my life. Fill me up with the Holy Spirit so that I am fully equipped to do every good work You've created for me to do. I pray You get Your glory in and through my life. Allow my life to be a testimony for all those who see Your great work in my life. In Jesus's name I pray, amen."

Reflection:

- After reading today's devotional, what is one thing God is saying to you?

- What does Ephesians 4:1 mean to you?

- What do you sense God is calling you to do? Have you received any confirmation? Write it down.

- Write down any other thoughts you have.

- Meditate on Ephesians 4:1 today.

DAY 3

A Challenge to Authenticity

Behold, I stand at the door, and knock. If anyone hears my voice and opens the door, I will come in to him, and will eat with him, and he with me.

—Revelation 3:20 (English Standard Version)

G od wants to talk to you. God wants you to be in His presence every single day. He desires that we live for Him; no lukewarm living but the kind of living that shows you're committed to Him. He wants you to be all the way when it comes to choosing Him. He wants your love and dedication.

Imagine a door in front of you. Imagine God on the other side of it knocking. Have you ever heard His knock? That knock is God calling your name. God is not going to open the door after he knocks. He is a gentleman. *You must open the door.* He will never force Himself in.

You must open the door.

Maybe God is tugging at your heart right now. Maybe God is knocking at your door. Possibly that is why you decided to pick up this devotional. Maybe He is tugging at your heart because your addiction needs to go, your habits need improvement, your thoughts need rewiring, or you need to make a

U-turn in your life. Whatever the reason, know He cannot help you make whatever change you need to make in your life until you open the door and let Him in every single room of your life. He wants to help you with the mess in your life. He wants to help clean you up. He wants to wipe away your tears. He wants to guide you through every single trial and difficulty you face.

My friend, God loves you and wants you to know His will concerning things for your life. God wants to speak to you. He wants to show you things about yourself and the abundant life He has promised for you. He's knocking. Do you hear Him? Would you invite Him in?

Prayer: "Lord, I hear You knocking on the door of my life. There are habits in my life that need to go. My thoughts need rewiring. I need to let go of the things that are weighing me down. I need a renovation, and I know you are the only one who can help me get one. Lord, I invite you in. I choose to open the door today and be in your presence. Please forgive me of my sins and help me make choices to change my life for the better. In Jesus's name I pray, amen."

Reflection:

- After reading today's devotional, what is one thing God is saying to you?

- What does Revelation 3:20 mean to you?

- Is God knocking on your door? Are there any areas of your life that need some fixing? How can you demonstrate that you trust God enough to open your door and invite His presence today?

- Write down any other thoughts you have.

- Meditate on Revelation 3:20 today.

DAY 4

Leave It Behind

Forget the former things; do not dwell on the past. See, I am doing a new thing! Now it springs up; do you not perceive it? I am making a way in the wilderness and streams in the wasteland.

—Isaiah 43:18–19 (New International Version)

Sometimes, I fall asleep playing an audio version of a person reading the Word of God. On one night in the middle of my sleep, I suddenly woke up to this passage, Isaiah 43:18–19. I was so amazed that God had allowed me to sleep throughout the night but specifically wake up to this passage—a passage that had been shared with me multiple times before this occurrence. When this happened, I knew it could only be God trying to get my attention and reveal to me how important and relevant this passage was to me. At that time of my life, God was doing a *new thing* in my life—a supernatural breakthrough. A miracle blessing was awaiting me.

My friend, I want you to know that God is a God of *newness*. He is a God of *new beginnings*. When you were saved, you entered the *new life* God has for all His children who put their trust in Him. If you desire to know the destiny God has for you and long to hear what He has to say to direct you into this destiny, you *must* leave yesterday behind. Starting something new can be difficult, whether it is a new relationship, a new job, or a new move to a different city; every new thing comes with great uncertainty and may require you to prepare yourself mentally, physically, or spiritually.

If God is moving you away from something, don't go back to it. Don't go back to something familiar, just because it feels comfortable. The focus should never be to get back to the "good old days'" and relive your best days in your past. Leave it behind. You're headed to something new, something great, something big, something miraculous. Move forward in faith to the unknown new thing God is doing, even if it feels uncomfortable, because sometimes stepping into the new thing feels scary. Sometimes you even may feel hesitant stepping into the new thing because you are still holding on to the regret and shame of your past. But today, I challenge you to let it go and move forward. God's mercies are new every morning and are so great to cleanse you of all your sins, mistakes, errors, and regrets. You may have wished you had not done a particular thing, *but* "in all things God works for the good of those who love Him, who have been called according to His purpose" (Romans 8:28, New International Version). Do you believe this promise? Look at the men in the Bible whose lives were full of so many regrets and mistakes, yet God was able to turn their mistakes into a message, their test into a testimony, and their mess into a masterpiece. Even the ones who messed up terribly; when they turned from their wicked ways and placed themselves under the mighty hand of God once again, God was able to miraculously turn their lives around and allow them to be a blessing to many others. Want proof?

Look at Moses, David, Jacob, Paul, and so many other warriors in the Bible. So yes, even your mistakes can help usher you into the destiny God has for you. God can use everything you face to get His

> *You're headed to something new, something great, something big, something miraculous.*

glory into your life. And even if you did not cause the mess in your life, God can take what the enemy meant for evil and turn it around for good, just like He did for Joseph.

God's good plan for you will always prevail if you just submit to Him. Trust God to do a *new thing* in your life, your marriage, your finances, your work, your relationships, your health, and whatever else you need His mighty hands to transform into new.

What God has in store for you does not compare to what you are letting go of—to what you are leaving behind. It's better up ahead. I promise.

Prayer: "Lord, You promised me that in all things You work for the good of those who love You and are called according to Your purpose. I believe You are doing a new thing in my life. I believe You are turning all my mess into a miracle. I believe You are allowing every test I have faced to be my testimony. I pray You to forgive me of my sins and help me to move forward into the new life You have in front of me. Remove the heavyweight of my sin, regrets, and past mistakes that are causing me to be stagnant. Align my heart's desire with Yours so that I can receive all that You have for me in this new life. In Jesus's name I pray, amen."

Reflection:

- After reading today's devotional, what is one thing God is saying to you?

- What does Isaiah 43:18–19 mean to you?

- Is there anything in your life that you are still holding on to that needs to go? What are some ways you can sense God doing a *new thing* in your life (or what are some new things you are trusting God to do in your life)?

- Write down any other thoughts you have.

- Meditate on Isaiah 43:18–19 today.

DAY 5

New Beginnings

Therefore, if anyone is in Christ, the new creation has come: The old has gone, the new is here!

—2 Corinthians 5:17 (New International Version)

Sometimes, when I think of the phrase, "new beginnings," I think of the term, "New Year's resolutions." A resolution is a firm decision to do something or not to do something. It is a promise to do something or not do something that you've determined in your mind and heart or have spoken out loud that you will do. Every January, New Year's resolutions begin with confidence and hope to reach our goals, but by the end of the year, most of us have forgotten what we promised ourselves we would or would not do. Many of us make them at the start of the new year, and many of us break them in the same year we make them. New Year's resolutions could include exercising at the gym, eating less junk food, becoming more financially responsible, practicing better self-care, spending more time with family, spending more time reading, or spending more time with God.

There is truly something satisfying and exciting about beginning a new year with a new resolution to fulfill that gives us a chance to get a fresh start in life, redeem our past year, and hope for new things to come. But what is the point if we do not carry through with this new thing that we are destined to do? Breaking New Year's resolutions is disappointing, but quite normal. It is our human nature to not follow through with our promises sometimes. But let me tell you about the One who can keep every single promise He has ever made. Let me tell you about the One who can do every single thing He has said He would do and help you to carry out the things He desires for you to do! God is the One. And He is the only One who is always doing a *new thing*! God not only always keeps His Word, but He is always giving His children a fresh word, a fresh start, and a fresh promise to new things to come.

> *God not only always keeps His Word, but He is always giving His children a fresh word, a fresh start, and a fresh promise to new things to come.*

As you continue your walk with Christ, I encourage you to choose to look to God as the source of *new things*. No matter how dark the journey, how many years you've been stuck in the same pattern, or how deep the pain appears to be in your life, believe that the best is yet to come. As you trust in Him, read the Word, and cling to His promises, day after day, you will begin to be transformed into the person God has purposed for you to be.

Prayer: "Lord, I believe you are a God of new things. I believe in the promises you have already given me in Your Word, that You will never leave or forsake me, that You are in control, that You are good, and that You have forgiven me of my sins. Lord, I rejoice because You are always doing new things in the lives of your children. I pray that you do a new thing in my life. I pray that you speak to me and show me the way in which I should go so that I see the new thing you are doing. Guide me so that I walk in the path You have set for me and experience all You have in store for me. Hold my hand as I live out the destiny You have given me. In Jesus's name I pray, amen."

Reflection:

- After reading today's devotional, what is one thing God is saying to you?

- What does 2 Corinthians 5:17 mean to you?

• What are some new ways God has changed your life as you have sought a relationship with Him? What are some new ways you can honor God today as He continues to mold you into the image of His Son?

• Write down any other thoughts you have.

• Meditate on 2 Corinthians 5:17.

DAY 6

Faith That Lasts

Truly I tell you, if anyone says to this mountain, "Go, throw yourself into the sea," and does not doubt in their heart but believes that what they say will happen, it will be done for them.

—Mark 11:23 (New International Version)

In July of 2020, my faith was tested so hard. That month, my sister, Hope, who had been battling cancer for almost two years in and out of the hospital, was in an unresponsive state. She had no consciousness or cognitive function. The day I found out she had entered this state, I was sitting on my living room couch, drinking a cup of water. I began to cry thinking the worst as I drank this cup of water, trying to calm myself down. In my head, I told myself, "I give up." As I was thinking this, I just so happened to look down and noticed the cup I was drinking from had the word "HOPE" on it. Immediately I realized God was speaking, and I began to encourage myself to believe and trust God to heal her. Tears streamed down my face when moments later, I came across a video by a preacher named Jerry Flowers, who talked about the power of God to heal and resurrect just as He did for Lazarus. Though Jerry did not know what I was going through, it felt as if God was speaking through him, reminding me of who He is; Jehovah-Rapha: The God Who

Heals. I continued to pray each night over Hope's body and for God to work a miracle and wake her up, even though the doctors thought otherwise. According to the doctors, she had already left; she was gone, and that was just her body on the bed. They informed my family that it was best for them to just pull the plug because things were not going to change.

Despite what the doctors had said, God kept stirring up in me the faith to believe a miracle would take place. I determined in my mind, not to give up on God. I prayed and visualized her waking up and greeting me with "Hey, Faith." Almost a week went by, and by the grace of God, Hope woke up, and her very first words were "Hey, Faith." I was so overwhelmed with joy and comfort at the happening of this miracle! That unforgettable day sparked an increase in my faith in God, Jehovah-Rapha, our Healer. My friend, anything is possible for one who believes. Our power and authority through Christ allow us to speak directly to obstacles and doubts of life and get them to move! Even faith the size of a mustard seed can move mountains!

Anything is possible for one who believes.

Through faith in Jesus, we have access to divine and healing power.

Maybe there is some obstacle in your life you desire God to remove. Maybe there is a problem in your life that needs fixing. Be honest with God about your circumstances and doubts and proceed in faith. Ask God to help your unbelief if you are struggling to trust Him. God will honor your faith and strengthen you despite your doubts and fears. Demonstrate faith by acting. Visualize your situation getting better. Visualize God doing a new and better thing in your life. The miracle God performed in my sister's life will always be a testimony I will never forget. Though my dear sister passed away after battling cancer, her healing, journey, and victory through all her tribulations will always be a testament to God's never-ending power and love for his children. God, Jehovah-Rapha, the God of the Old Testament and New Testament, is the same God today who still has the power to heal our diseases. And He can do more than we ask, think, or imagine! Believe in the impossible, my friend, and watch Him perform a miracle in your life.

Prayer: "God, I believe you are Jehovah-Rapha, the God who heals. God, you created me. You know and understand my needs. You know my thoughts even before I may speak them. Father, I ask now that You come to my need and deliver me. I ask for Your divine power and healing. Lord, I believe You have the power to heal, and I pray for that power to enter my body and heal me. I pray You not only heal physically, but I pray You do a deep work, deep down on the inside, cleansing my heart and renewing my mind. Allow Your healing to flow on me like a living stream. Help me to trust in Your power in my weakness. Show me what You are trying to teach me in this suffering. Sustain me by Your grace. Help me to rest in You and engage my faith as I wait on You to perform this work in my life. May my life be a testament to Your healing power. Do the impossible through me. In Jesus's name, amen."

Reflection:

- After reading today's devotional, what is one thing God is saying to you?

- What does Mark 11:23 mean to you?

- How big or small is your faith? What are some things you can write down that can help you build your faith?

- Write down any other thoughts you have.

- Meditate on Mark 11:23 today.

"Thy Kingdom Come, Thy Will Be Done"

Thy kingdom come, Thy will be done in earth, as it is in heaven.

—Matthew 6:10 (King James Version)

The true goal of prayer is in the verse above. When we pray, we must ultimately ask for God's will to be done. Sometimes, when life gets overburdened with struggles, trials, and difficulties, our natural tendency is to focus on this all in our prayers. As we do this continually, we begin to lose focus of prayer as we run down our checklist of petitions and needs. Our prayers begin to lose substance as we focus only on what we need and desire. Petitions are certainly good, and the Bible tells us to let our requests be made known to our Lord God, but prayer is also a time that we have the privilege and opportunity to focus on God's kingdom.

In moments that we want to focus only on our needs, we must instead turn our focus toward God and His glorious kingdom. When praying, we should always pray for God's kingdom to come and for His will to be done. In other words, we should acknowledge God's reign and submit to His kingdom authority over our lives.

Understanding God's kingdom and God's will is the key to living with purpose because all our lives are tied to God's kingdom and what He wills and desires for us. When we pray, we must never forget to focus on the main reason for prayer. We must pray for God's will to be done even if it is not in alignment with our own will. And when we focus on God and His will more than on our troubles, God will begin to change our hearts about our situation.

Moreover, we must always aim to express our gratitude and love for God as we pray. This is another goal of prayer; the praise and exaltation of our God should happen when we pray. It is a shame to go from day to day without acknowledging and praising God for being the source of your life. God is the reason for our existence; He is the source of the breath and life we have. Prayer allows us to express to God how we feel about Him, how much we need Him, and how there is no one else above Him.

We should never fail to give glory and praise that He is due in prayer. When we create a lifestyle of thanksgiving and praise as we pray, we will experience God in a whole new and different way. It's about God's name, God's kingdom, and God's will. Make prayer about Him.

It's about God's name, God's kingdom, and God's will.

Prayer: "God, I trust in You. You have the final say on everything in my life. Lord, I pray for Your kingdom to come and Your will to be done, even if it is different than what I desire. You are a good God. Your ways are not my ways; Your thoughts are not my thoughts. I believe in Your authority to work out circumstances in this world and in my life that bring You the greatest glory. I believe You know how to answer my prayers in a way that will allow You to get the greatest glory in my life. You are working even when I do not see it. Lord, allow me to patiently wait on You as you perform miracles out of my mess. Thank You for Your overflow of favor, goodness, and unending grace in my life. In Jesus's name, amen."

Reflection:

- After reading today's devotional, what is one thing God is saying to you?

- What does Matthew 6:10 mean to you?

- What are some things God is speaking to you about, concerning His will for your life? Is it different or similar to your thoughts, plans, or desires? Do you trust God enough to declare for His will to be done in your life, even if it is different from your own will and desire?

- Write down any other thoughts you have.

- Meditate on Matthew 6:10 today.

DAY 8

Cry Out to God

This poor man cried, and the Lord heard him, and saved him out of all his troubles.

—Psalm 34:6 (King James Version)

One day, God allowed the scripture reference, Psalm 34:6 to be placed on my mind. It wasn't like this reference was a verse I memorized growing up, or repeated time and time again at Sunday school. I had never read this verse before, and I could not understand why this reference was on my mind. It was almost like the Holy Spirit just laid this reference on my heart. I did not know the words in this verse, so I immediately went to my Bible, searched it, and read it to myself. The very next day I did what I normally do every day—check my email. But this day was different from other days. On this day when I checked my email, I received a devotional from Charles Stanley with the verse Psalm 34:6. This devotional was about crying out to God in faith in times of desperation. At that moment, I knew God was speaking to me. He was trying to get my attention to recognize the power contained in this verse. This verse showed me that God is a God that not only hears us when we cry out to Him, but He is a God who delivers us and saves us from all our troubles.

He is a God who delivers us and saves us from all our troubles.

With prayer, patience, and perseverance, we will begin to see God change things in our lives as we cry out to Him. If you have cried out to God about an issue, do not give up. Just as a woman giving birth pushes and pushes until she sees or hears her newborn baby cries, seek God's face until you hear Him speak. Push prayers out of your mouth until you begin to see God start to move in your situation and perform a miracle in your life. Pray until you get an answer. Cry out until you feel His touch. Labor spiritually until you see God's hand at work in your life. God is already working, even when we cannot see things changing. That's what I love about God. He is a silent worker. But it also takes work on our part to see in the physical what God had been doing all along in the spiritual. Our work is prayer. Our work is fasting. Our work is praising God until we get a breakthrough! Be persistent and keep going until God delivers you! "The effectual fervent prayer of a righteous man availeth much" (James 5:16, King James Version). Your answer is just a prayer away.

Prayer: "God, I cry out to You in desperate faith. I thank You for not just hearing my cries of trouble, but I thank You that you are my God who is capable and has all power to deliver me from my troubles. Thank You for being my Provider. Thank You for being my Protector. Thank You for being my Healer. Thank You for being my Deliver. Lord, You know my thoughts. You know exactly what I am dealing with. I pray that You provide for my needs and bring me out of this trial with a testimony. Turn my mess into a message that I can share with people to tell of Your goodness, mercy, favor, and grace. I trust You will provide for my every need, whether it is a job, finances, healing, or so much more than I could have ever imagined. I trust Your power. I trust in Your provision. Lord, deliver me and change me so that I see what You see and think thoughts of You. In Jesus's name, amen."

Reflection:

- After reading today's devotional, what is one thing God is saying to you?

- What does Psalm 34:6 mean to you?

- Is there anything you are crying out for God to do in your life? Write it down. Do you believe He can deliver you?

- Write down any other thoughts you have.

- Meditate on Psalm 34:6 today.

DAY 9

Think on Things Above

Set your minds on things above, not on earthly things.

—Colossians 3:2 (New International Version)

O ne day as I was driving, the passage Colossians 3 started playing randomly in my car. I was so confused and began to try to figure out what was going on. I then noticed my phone was connected to the Apple CarPlay, but I was still puzzled as to how it had begun playing scripture out of nowhere. I looked around on my phone and noticed the Bible app was open on my phone and realized that this passage was playing from the Bible app. Still to this day, I do not recall how my Bible app went to this direct passage, but that day changed my life, and since that moment, I have repeatedly meditated on this passage.

This passage focuses on Christ's desire for us to think about heavenly things instead of things happening on this earth. In other words, since our minds determine our well-being and how we live our lives every day, we must center our hearts and minds on Christ and the things of God. When we do this, we begin to receive everything that we need for daily living, which ultimately brings us peace and purpose in this life. As we continue to do this daily,

God begins to change our hearts, minds, and lives and enables us to blossom into beautiful gardens. But on the other hand, when we place too much of our focus on worldly things, our lives suddenly spiral into a whirlwind of disorder, disaster, and wreck. We lose focus of what truly matters.

To live a life full of purpose and one that glorifies God, we must shift our focus daily and have a heavenly mind-set for the daily earthly actions we take. In doing this, we will remain at the center of God's will and be able to get heaven's perspective and God's opinion of every single situation and issue that arises on earth. Setting our minds on things above will enable us to not only receive God's opinion on our personal matters, but it will enable us to put off our old ways (the sinful ways we engaged in before we knew Christ) and embrace this new life that God has given us through salvation in Jesus Christ. In Christ, we have a new identity and must put off our old ways and sinful habits: anger, rage, malice, slander, filthy language, lying, and other old ways and practices. Instead, we are to be clothed with compassion, kindness, humility, gentleness, and patience. We must also aim to forgive others as we put on this new self, given to us through our relationship with Christ.

Choose to let God elevate your heart to where Christ is. In doing this, you will experience His love, grace, kindness, hope, peace, joy, and goodness to help you on this journey of faith.

Choose to let God elevate your heart to where Christ is.

Prayer: "God, I thank You for Your death on the cross for my sins and resurrection from the tomb that has allowed me to be able to experience a relationship with You and be forgiven and cleansed of all my sins. I pray that as I focus my heart and mind on heavenly things, You will begin to change me and conform me to the image of your Son. As I follow Your ways and path for my life, I pray that You will help me to have an eternal mind-set, one that focuses on glorifying you in all that I do and say. Give me wisdom and the strength to prepare for eternity as I live for You now. If I ever turn my focus off of You, help me to center it back on You and Your purpose, plan, and will for my life. In Jesus's name, amen."

Reflection:

- After reading today's devotional, what is one thing God is saying to you?

- What does Colossians 3:2 mean to you?

- What dominates your thoughts? Are you more concerned with the things of Christ or worldly and material things on earth?

- Write down any other thoughts you have.

- Meditate on Colossians 3:2 today.

God Directs My Life, I'm Just Keeping the Faith

"For I know the plans I have for you," declares the Lord, "plans to prosper you and not to harm you, plans to give you hope and a future."

—Jeremiah 29:11 (New International Version)

In preparation for my graduation day, my late sister, Hope, designed and decorated my graduation cap with the words:

"God Directs My Life, I'm Just
Keeping the Faith"

Fast-forward four years. I was sitting on my bed one night thinking to myself, "I don't think I am in my right lane." That morning I opened my daily devotional called "Called for a Purpose," by Tony Evans, to a page titled, "Motivation in the Mundane." To my surprise, in his very first few sentences, Tony Evans wrote, "One of the reasons many of us are unfulfilled is that we are driving in the wrong lane. We operate in lanes in life that were never intended for us. We operate for purposes that were never designed for us." At that moment I knew God was trying to get my attention. I prayed to God and asked Him to "help me take the right exit," and that night He revealed to me in a dream the vision and purpose He had for my life. I woke up blown away and inspired. I was then reminded of the words my sister designed on my cap: "God Directs My Life, I'm Just Keeping the Faith." I had believed in faith for God to show me the right exit to take, and on that same day, He had directed my life by giving me a glimpse of my future in a dream.

My friend, I encourage you to keep the faith as God directs your daily life. Yes, some moments will feel mundane, slow-paced, and silent, but God is at work. Remember, He is a silent worker. Even when we don't see Him, He is working. And when His work is revealed, you will see it was worth *Even when we don't see* the wait. My friend, my prayer is that *Him, He is working.* you will look to God as your source and guide so that He can help you take the right exit. It would be a shame for you to miss the purpose and plan God has for your life by not submitting to Him and acknowledging Him as your Shepherd and daily guide. Do not take the wrong exit and go the opposite way of the intended destination God has for you. God will give you all you need plus more so that you can carry out with perseverance and motivation the purpose He has for your life. Today, ask God to show you His will. Ask Him to give you a glimpse of what is to come. If He did it for me, He can do it for you.

Prayer: "Lord, I need Your guidance. I want Your will. I trust You as my Shepherd. God, I want to honor You with all You have given me: my time, gifts, passions, talents, and resources. Help me develop the gifts and talents You have given me. Unleash my passion for You and the work You have given me as I fulfill my purpose as best as I can. Father, I pray that You show me the right exit to take in my life so that I journey on the path You have designed for me. You direct my life; I am just keeping the faith. Help me to focus on you and not get discouraged when things seem mundane and pointless in my life. Help me to stay motivated and determined to live out each day with intentionality. Lord, usher me into my purpose, my destiny, and the great calling you have planned for me. In Jesus's name, amen."

Reflection:

- After reading today's devotional, what is one thing God is saying to you?

- What does Jeremiah 29:11 mean to you?

- Do you see God moving in your life to bring into fruition the good plans and purpose He has for you? Are you struggling with doubt based on your current life situation right now? Do you have confidence in the great plans God has for you?

- Write down any other thoughts you have.

- Meditate on Jeremiah 29:11 today.

Divine Direction

Trust in the Lord with all thine heart; and lean not unto thine own understanding. In all thy ways acknowledge him, and he shall direct thy paths.

—Proverbs 3:5–6 (King James Version)

Many men of the Bible experienced divine encounters by God. Abraham encountered God on his way to obey God's command and sacrifice his son, Isaac. Jacob encountered God as he wrestled with him until daybreak. Peter encountered God as he walked on water. But these encounters didn't just happen by chance. These encounters happened as these men of the Bible put their trust in God. They trusted in the Lord and submitted themselves to His plan. They leaned on God instead of leaning on their own understanding. And thank God they didn't trust in their own ways.

Our thinking and understanding won't always support us. Only God's ways are truly dependable. And knowing God's ways will give us insight into His divine direction so that we walk in the path *Only God's ways are* He has designed for us and get to our *truly dependable.* intended destination. Who do you turn to first when calamity strikes? Who do you turn to first when you need help? Who do you turn to first for advice on your life's circumstances? If your answer is God, you are turning to the right One! God is the One we should turn to in whatever we face, little or big, because He is omniscient and has all wisdom.

As we walk righteously and please God in all that we do, God will make our paths straight. He has all power to remove any obstacles in our path that can deter us from the path He has designed for us. He will indeed make sure we get to our intended destination as we place our faith in Him. He knows the route we must take so that we live in the purpose He has designed for us. God's divine direction is the only direction that will allow us to live out the plan and purpose we were created for. To begin to receive divine direction, we must read the Word of God and pray so that God can begin to reveal the path He has for us—a path that may be quite different from the path that we made for ourselves. But when we begin to trust God and walk in faith, we will understand that His path is way better than our path could ever be. His thoughts and plans are higher than ours. As we follow Christ and acknowledge God in all our ways, He will direct us on the good path that He designed for us. As we live in faith, God will show us the divine direction we need so that we will live out our true purpose, help lead souls to Christ, give God the glory He is due, and receive every single blessing He has for us.

Prayer: "Lord, I need Your divine direction. Make my path straight as I acknowledge You in all that I do. I believe that as I walk in integrity, You will make my journey straight, no matter the road curves. I want You to direct my life so that I follow your perfect will and plan. Lord, I look to You today to allow me to encounter You in a whole new way. I desire a personal experience with You just as the men and women of the Bible experienced You. Show me Yourself. Draw near to me as I draw near to You. Lord, change my life as I submit to Your way. If I am going in the wrong direction, redirect my path. Give me a divine encounter with You that will take me above the ordinary and normal into the extraordinary and supernatural so that I reach a new level in You. In Jesus's name, amen."

Reflection:

- After reading today's devotional, what is one thing God is saying to you?

- What does Proverbs 3:5–6 mean to you?

- Have you ever had a divine encounter with God? Write it down. What are some areas of your life you need to surrender over to God so He can direct your paths?

- Write down any other thoughts you have.

- Meditate on Proverbs 3:5–6 today.

DAY 12

Gracefully Broken

So Jacob was left alone, and a man wrestled with him till daybreak. When the man saw that he could not overpower him, he touched the socket of Jacob's hip so that his hip was wrenched as he wrestled with the man. Then the man said, "Let me go, for it is daybreak. But Jacob replied, "I will not let you go unless you bless me."

—Genesis 32:24–26 (New International Version)

Jacob said, "Please tell me your name." But he replied, "Why do you ask my name?" Then he blessed him there.

—Genesis 32:29 (New International Version)

In 2021, I had a dream of a man walking with a limp. When I woke up from this dream, I began to think of the story of Jacob and the event that caused him to walk with a limp. If you don't know this story of Jacob, let me tell it to you. In Genesis 22, we learn about Jacob and the meaning of his name. His name means deceiver or trickster. Jacob fit his name very well. He was born a deceiver, exemplified through how he came out of his mother's womb grabbing his brother Esau's heel. Later, we find out that he tricks Esau and steals his birthright. Esau becomes angry, and to avoid retaliation from his brother, Jacob flees his home, family, and all that he ever knew. But then God steps in. And we know that when God steps in in any situation, something is bound to change. In Genesis 32, Jacob comes to a dreadful crisis. After years of living far away from his brother, he must leave in obedience to God's command, realizing he will have to face his brother again. Though God promises to be with Jacob, Jacob fears that his brother is going to kill him because of his deceitful actions toward him in the past. As he is on his way, Jacob finds some time to get away, alone. He feels helpless and stripped of any protection. What happens next? He is left alone and begins to wrestle a stranger who appears. He wrestles with this man throughout the night. When the man sees that Jacob isn't giving up, he touches the socket of Jacob's thigh so that it becomes wrenched. He then tells Jacob to let him go. Jacob, knowing this was God Himself who had twisted his hip, responds by saying, "I will not let you go unless you bless me." This response showed Jacob's perseverance even amid the struggle. When God is trying to change you, He may allow difficult situations in your life. But as we see here in Jacob's example, there is a blessing tied to the breaking. Sometimes God allows us to be broken but gracefully. And just like Jacob did, when we break from the crisis of life, we must hold on to the One who can put us back together. When life puts us through twists and turns, we must hold on to God's unchanging hand. We must hold on until we get our breakthrough—until we get our blessing. What prompted Jacob's request for God's blessing is his understanding of the man he was wrestling with. Jacob knew he wasn't dealing with any ordinary man. He was dealing with God. God responds to Jacob's question to bless him by saying, "What is your name?" In other words, God wanted Jacob to be real with Him and tell Him who he was—a deceiver, a trickster. That is what Jacob was. Now, my friend, your name might not be Jacob, but maybe you have similar habits like him. Maybe you are a deceiver, liar, or thief. Maybe your name is lust, doubt, or fear. Whatever your name is, just know God can do just what He did for Jacob—change your name. Not only did God change Jacob's name to Israel, but he blessed him there in the same spot Jacob wrestled with Him. God did a spiritual work in Jacob's life and, my friend, He can do one in yours too. What is that struggle in your life that is causing distance between you and God? What is keeping God from giving you all that He has already promised you? For Jacob, it was his name—his deceit, his trickster ways. Maybe for you, it is your addiction. Or maybe it is your pride. Maybe it is your dependence on material things, such as your house, car, or money?

Any idol that causes humans to deny the provision and mercy of God in their lives is also the reason for any distance that could exist between them and God. God knows you. He sees you and will allow circumstances, difficulties, and trials over His providential hand to disrupt your life for you to change from the inside out. Sometimes God lets our lives fall apart to help us realize He is the only one we can truly depend on and trust to put it back together, in a completely new and better way.

Sometimes God allows sickness, loss of a job, financial struggles, or even broken relationships to strip us of any dependence on ourselves, people, and earthly things so that He can change our character and mold us into the image of His Son. So let God change your name, my friend. For God to change your name, He must break you from your past. So keep wrestling through your trials for Him to break you to make you. On the other side of your brokenness is your breakthrough. On the other side of your pain is your blessing.

On the other side of your brokenness is your breakthrough. On the other side of your pain is your blessing.

Prayer: "Lord, I rely on You as my strength. Even during dark moments when it feels as if You are not here, I believe You are here watching over me and providing for me. I pray You reveal to me the purpose of my life and reveal what You are teaching me in the valley. I pray that my test would be turned into a testimony and any mess in my life will allow me to one day have a message to share with people of Your goodness, favor, and grace. Hide me in the shadow of Your wings and protect me from falling into temptation as I walk in Your perfect way. I trust Your will and ways. Get Your glory in and through me. In Jesus's name, amen."

- After reading today's devotional, what is one thing God is saying to you?

- What does Genesis 32:24–26 and Genesis 32:29b mean to you?

- What does the phrase "gracefully broken," mean to you? In what ways have you been gracefully broken? Do you feel like giving up or are you determined to wrestle like Jacob?

- Write down any other thoughts you have.

- Meditate on Genesis 32:24–26 and Genesis 32:29b today.

The Process of Brokenness

Not only so, but we also glory in our sufferings, because we know that suffering produces perseverance; perseverance, character; and character, hope. And hope does not put us to shame, because God's love has been poured out into our hearts through the Holy Spirit, who has been given to us.

—Romans 5:3–5 (New International Version)

B roken is just where God wants you to be. It is God's requirement for maximum usefulness. Brokenness allows God to use us to our fullest potential. Because He desires that we reach spiritual wholeness and grow in our character, He will use tribulations, trials, betrayals, and even affliction from the enemy to break our dependence on anything other than Him. God may allow physical suffering, emotional pain, relationship hurt, disappointment, and other painful situations to bring you closer to Him. When God allows us to go through painful situations, the best thing we can do is cling to Him as our hope.

You are exactly where God wants you to be if you are in a difficult situation right now.

You are exactly where God wants you to be if you are in a difficult situation right now. Everything that happens in our lives must first pass through God's almighty hands. The process of being broken will take you from brokenness to bitterness, but in the end, you will experience a breakthrough. In the end, you will receive God's blessing He has always had in store for you. In the end, you will become *brand new*. And when you do, you will know you can never be dependent on anyone or anything other than God! You will know that God is your strength in your weakness, and there is no one else who can carry you as He can.

Let God break you to make you. Let him develop and shake you. Let God strip you of your pride and self-sufficiency so you can experience Him for who He truly is. Let God mold you into the person He has designed for you to be. Let Him be your Shepherd so that you can walk in the purpose He has called for you to walk in. Life will never be the same once you decide to submit to God and the purpose He has for your life. And God can use everything in your life for your good and His glory.

If you are feeling the burden and pain of the circumstances that you may be enduring right now, I need you to know that God cares for you, my friend. He loves you and wants the best for you. There is no good thing that He will withhold from those who walk in His righteous way. My friend, I also encourage you to ask God to reveal what He is teaching you. Allow His power, grace, and holy presence to sustain you as you mature into the man or woman that He desires you to be. As you abide in Him, He will begin to give you a new perspective of your current circumstance, and His mercy and grace will allow you to receive strength, perseverance, patience, and provision to endure the trials of life.

Prayer: "Lord, carry me through the burdens and struggles of life. Though life's trials and difficulties may cause me to be broken, and my brokenness can sometimes lead me to become bitter, I trust that I will come out of this test with a breakthrough. I pray that You will use every single thing I have been through for Your good. I know the enemy will not win, and I will receive everything You have already promised me. Lord, help me to wait on You as my heart is transformed. I believe my blessing is on the way, so I will praise You in advance! Thank You for being a good God. I trust in You. In Jesus's name, amen."

Reflection:

- After reading today's devotional, what is one thing God is saying to you?

- What does Romans 5:3–5 mean to you?

- Do you feel you are being broken? What are some things you can do as you walk through the process of brokenness to demonstrate your trust in God?

- Write down any other thoughts you have.

- Meditate on Romans 5:3–5 today.

DAY 14

All for a Purpose

And we know that in all things God works for the good of those who love him, who have been called according to his purpose.

—Romans 8:28 (New International Version)

As my sister, Hope, battled cancer, she always had our father, Michael Wells, by her side to uplift and encourage her. One night in her hospital room, God spoke through my father who told Hope, "God will use this for good." He encouraged her to have faith to believe God would use her story to touch the lives of many watching her as she battled this illness. As they were chatting it up, a nurse came into the room to move them into another room so Hope could receive her chemotherapy. As they entered this new room, they saw a book on a table, titled *God Will Use This for Good*," by Max Lucado. Their faces brightened, and they smiled.

This personal story and many other stories from the life of my sister always reminds me to keep hope alive in whatever trial or disappointment I face. Why? Because God can use it for good. Whenever you face adversity, pray, and walk with confidence and faith that God will use what you are going through for good. Not only will God's peace overtake you as you trust in Him to use all your trials, difficulties, struggles, and even mistakes for good, but when you allow God to guide you through your circumstances, He will allow your adversity to be turned into an opportunity. He did it for Daniel when he was thrown into the lions' den for his faith. He did it for Shadrach, Meshach, and Abednego when they were thrown into a fiery furnace for choosing to honor God and refusing to bow to King Nebuchadnezzar. And God can do it for you.

He will allow your adversity to be turned into an opportunity.

When you're going through challenging situations, you can lose sight of who God is. In tough times, you can get discouraged and start to fall away. I know this because I've experienced this. But I urge you today if this is you who has begun to fall away, come back to the Father. God loves you, and He always will. He has a great plan and great things in store for you. When hard moments and threats come your way, choose to walk this life of faith with patience and consistent prayer. Not only will God allow your trial to bring you closer to Him, but He will use it for good! Be open to what God is teaching you whenever you face trials of many kinds. God has never shut the door of His miracle-making business, so allow Him to do a miracle in your life.

Prayer: "Lord, life can sometimes feel overwhelming with all the adversity I face. Help me to look to You whenever I feel the weight of giving up. Let Your guiding hand cover me and Your wings carry me like an eagle's wings carries its young ones. I know You are making me stronger and wiser with each test and battle I overcome. Lord, I believe You are a good God who can use my pain for a purpose. Thank You for Your promise that You can use everything in my life, the good and the bad, for good. In Jesus's name, amen."

Reflection:

- After reading today's devotional, what is one thing God is saying to you?

- What does Romans 8:28 mean to you?

- Is there a difficult trial or disappointment right now? Do you believe God can work it out for your good? How can you demonstrate your trust in God's power to turn your mess into a miracle?

- Write down any other thoughts you have.

- Meditate on Romans 8:28 today.

Wait on the Lord

> But those who wait on the Lord shall renew their strength; they shall mount up with wings like eagles, they shall run and not be weary, they shall walk and not faint.
>
> **—Isaiah 40:31 (New King James Version)**

At the beginning of 2020, I was single. I can clearly remember one night thinking to myself, "Can God expedite the process of marriage?" I then began to search this exact question on google and could not find a single answer.

The next day, as I was listening to a preacher on YouTube, he began talking about marriage and how the process of marriage cannot be expedited, but instead, one must get into position for it. I was stunned, shocked, and blown away by the fact that God had allowed me to receive the answer to this question so quickly. He helped me to understand that being in position allows me to be ready to receive what God already has in store for me. If I am out of position, things and events could be delayed. Instead of trying to rush my life and the plans God has for me, I must wait on the Lord.

When I think of waiting, I also think of one of the fruits of the Spirit, patience. Patience involves waiting but goes beyond and above just waiting. Patience is "waiting well." Patience could involve you praying as you wait. Patience could involve you praising God as you wait. Patience could involve you encouraging yourself as you wait. Patience could involve serving others while you wait. Patience is not just sitting like you are at a bus stop waiting for a blessing to drop flat on your lap. Patience involves you acting as you wait.

Maybe you are not waiting for a spouse like me (or maybe you are; we are in this together, my friend, lol), but maybe you are waiting for a job or a raise. Maybe you are waiting for a house or a car. Maybe you are waiting for a relationship to be restored. Maybe you are waiting for your child to start behaving better. Maybe you are waiting for healing. Maybe you are waiting to be debt-free. Maybe you are waiting on clarity and wisdom from God on where to move next. Whatever it is that you are currently waiting on God to do in your life, know that He is also waiting for you. He is waiting for you to be in position to receive the miracle He has already promised you.

As you wait, I encourage you to imitate Hannah's position in the Bible. Hannah desired so strongly to have a child, but she struggled with infertility. One day, she prayed to God for a child and promised to dedicate her child to Him if He would answer her prayer. Hannah laid aside her desires and decided to surrender to the Lord's will, and the Lord opened her wound. Like Hannah, I encourage you to submit your desire to God and wait on Him. My friend, wait on God, and let Him prepare you for His promise for you. When we get tired of waiting for the Lord, go in a direction opposite of His will, and rush ahead of Him because we are tired of waiting, we risk missing out on the blessings He has in store for us. Timing is everything to God, so hold on to patience. God has blessings for you to enjoy, so wait well. God will never change His mind about His promises and plans in store for you. Not only will He give you the desires

Timing is everything to God, so hold on to patience.

- 71 -

of your heart if it is in alignment with His will, but He will do exceedingly abundantly, more than we can ask or even imagine.

Prayer: "Lord, I come before You with my heart full of thoughts and concerns about my life. Lord, help me to wait on You as I walk through the uncertainties of my life. Lord, I trust in You to give me answers and direct my life so that I can walk in the purpose You have for me. Lord, help me through the doubts and fear that may arise as I ponder how long I will have to wait. Give me strength and grace to wait well instead of complaining about how long it is taking for You to move in my life. You are Sovereign and know exactly how to govern my life and this world You spoke into existence. Lord, I pray You speak to me as I wait on You. Reveal Yourself to me, and help me know You better. I place my trust in Your care and control. Forgive me for impatience and fear. Give me the perseverance to continue to seek Your face and trust You as I wait on You. In the precious name of Jesus, amen."

Reflection:

- After reading today's devotional, what is one thing God is saying to you?

- What does Isaiah 40:31 mean to you?

- What are you waiting on God to do in your life? What can you do as you practice patience in the wait?

- Write down any other thoughts you have.

- Meditate on Isaiah 40:31 today.

DAY 16

Obedience

If you love Me, keep My commands.

—John 14:15 (New King James Version)

In the beginning of 2022, God began tugging at my heart about obedience. I began to look to His Word to learn more about this action God requires from us in His Word. In God's Word, the subject of obedience is mentioned throughout the Old and New Testaments. In scripture, God instructs us to obey our parents as children, governing authorities, and above all, obey God.

In life, we all have choices, some more difficult than others. But regardless of what kind of choice life presents us, we should obey God at any cost. We must use the wisdom God freely gives to those who ask Him and obey God above all no matter how difficult the task in front of us may be. And sometimes the decision to obey God is difficult. Sometimes the decision to obey God results in rejection, hardship, ridicule, or even loss. However, our heavenly Father is good, omniscient, omnipotent, and faithful. Any choice He leads us to make always has a good reason behind it. All we must do is trust Him.

Disobedience, on the other hand, sends a message that we know better and are wiser than God. But we aren't. God's ways and thoughts are higher and better than ours. When He asks for our obedience, it is out of love for us. He does not want us to miss out on the great future He has for us, and

When He asks for our obedience, it is out of love for us.

trust me, my friend, God has great blessings and plans in store for us all— things we would have never imagined! To see these blessings, we must submit to Him. Repeatedly, day after day, we must choose to follow God's plan and directions for our lives laid out in His Word, even if it hurts. We must aim to seek His Word, and His voice will guide us to making decisions that will help us in our daily lives.

My friend, what choices are stacked in front of you as you walk this journey called life? Before making a decision, talk to God and get His opinion on the matter. And when you get His opinion, obey Him. Obeying God will allow you to receive His very best. It may appear difficult and hard at times, but in the end, complying with His will allows you to reap the rewards and benefits that come with being a believer and follower of Christ. And my friend, you'll never lose with Christ!

Prayer: "Lord, I trust You to help me as I tackle the unending questions and decisions in life. I pray that You help me to obey You no matter how hard the choice in front of me may be. Lead and guide me to make choices that reflect Your perfect will. Your will is best. Your plan is best. Your purpose for my life outshines any purpose I have made for myself. Help me to lean on You and trust in Your way. Help me to make better choices and grow in obedience to You. In Jesus's name, amen."

Reflection:

- After reading today's devotional, what is one thing God is saying to you?

- What does John 14:15 mean to you?

- What is God laying on your heart to do that you may find difficult? In what ways can you show your trust and love for God by obeying Him?

- Write down any other thoughts you have.

- Meditate on John 14:15 today.

DAY 17

God Can Still Use You

For we are God's handiwork, created in Christ Jesus to do good works, which God prepared in advance for us to do.

—Ephesians 2:10 (New International Version)

This devotion is for the hurt, the broken, the rejected, the folks who feel unlovable and unforgivable, the folks that are struggling with shame and regret from the past. I want you to know that you are beautifully and wonderfully made. You are created for a great purpose. You are not too far gone. *God can still use you.*

The pain of rejection weighed heavy on me during my last year of college. I had applied for a job in my field. I just knew I needed this new role I had just applied for to advance in my field. But I was rejected. It took me some time to get over this rejection. It would have been much easier to accept this rejection if it had been the first rejection email, but this felt like it was the thousandth time I had been told no by a company within my field. I was disappointed, sad, and on the brink of feeling hopeless. Despite the array of my feelings, I got on my knees that night and prayed. "Lord, use me; I give You my all, everything belongs to You, but just use me." I knew I had come to the end of myself when I said this prayer, but somewhere deep inside of me, I trusted that this was only the beginning of God doing something new in my heart. God began to move, and to my surprise, I was comforted the next morning when I received a devotional that talked about how God can use those who put their trust in Him.

My friend, I encourage you to believe that God can use you. Seek God and allow Him to be a priority in your life so that He can use you to your fullest potential. The best thing you can do in your Christian walk is surrender to God and allow God to give you direction, clarity, and purpose for your life. When you do this, God will begin to turn your situation around for your good and His glory! Yes, you may feel broken, but God can still use you! You may feel buried in shame, doubt,

God can still use you! or fear, but God can still use you! You may have experienced rejection after rejection after rejection, and you feel like throwing in the towel, but God can still use you! You may feel like the waiting never ends, but God can still use you! You may feel unforgivable, like all of God's grace has run out, but you can't exhaust God's endless supply of grace. God can still use you!

When you come to the end of yourself, ask God for His peace, strength, and provision to keep you going amid the storms and chaos in front of you. His presence will strengthen you in the storm, and His almighty power can command the chaos to be no more. You may not realize it, but everything you have faced—your trials, difficulties, and disappointments—can all be used for your good and God's glory. God will enable you to share everything you have learned and survived with someone else to encourage and strengthen them. And your testimony can help them get through what they are facing in life. Your testimony can help others overcome their fears and difficulties.

So choose to believe that God can use you.

Prayer: "Lord, sometimes the pain of life can beat me down. Sometimes my pain from the past can cause me to feel worthless and unworthy, but I believe in Your power to turn my pain into purpose. I believe You can still use me. I pray that You use my hurt, my struggles, my disappointments, and even my mistakes to get Your glory in my life. Turn my test into a testimony that will serve and benefit Your kingdom and lead souls to Christ. Walk beside me as I continue to endure life's challenges. Help me to put down the pen I've been using to write my own life's story and allow You all control to write my story. You direct my life, and I know that with You, I have the victory. In Jesus, amen."

Reflection:

- After reading today's devotional, what is one thing God is saying to you?

- What does Ephesians 2:10 mean to you?

- Do you believe that God can use you? In what ways and areas is God showing you He can use you?

- Write down any other thoughts you have.

- Meditate on Ephesians 2:10 today.

The Beauty of Grace

Then Peter came to Jesus and asked, "Lord, how many times shall I forgive my brother or sister who sins against me? Up to seven times?" Jesus answered, "I tell you, not seven times, but seventy-seven times."

—Matthew 18:21–22 (New International Version)

W e've all been hurt by one's actions or words at some point in our lives. Many of us have experienced bitterness, resentment, and even unforgiveness because of it. But if you stay stuck in these feelings, you'll begin to feel stuck in life. Jesus knows this, which is why He talks about the importance of forgiveness throughout the Bible. In the passage above, Jesus's intention was not to give an exact number of times we as believers should forgive, but His purpose was to show how necessary it is to practice forgiveness in our everyday lives. Why? Because there is power in forgiveness. There is freedom in forgiveness. There is healing in forgiveness. Too many times, believers fail to recognize this power, freedom, and healing that forgiveness brings. Instead, they choose to hold grudges, which causes them to grow bitter and stay stuck and stagnant.

In one season of my life, I was struggling with heavy bitterness I thought would never stop weighing me down. One night, I had a dream of the exact issue that was causing this bitterness. In this dream, God showed me exactly what I needed to do and who I needed to forgive to release myself of this bitterness. I woke up amazed and decided from that day forward that I would be intentional about letting God rid me of this unforgiveness and bitterness harboring in my heart. As I prayed to God, read devotionals, listened to sermons, and meditated on scripture, God began to work on my heart.

A newness comes with giving grace. Healing comes with giving grace. Freedom comes with giving grace. When we choose to obey God and give grace, God steps in and expedites the healing process. Though it may seem hard to forgive in the beginning, releasing the burden that comes with carrying hurt and pain will bring so much freedom and closeness with Christ.

A newness comes with giving grace. Healing comes with giving grace. Freedom comes with giving grace.

Choose forgiveness today. Choose to pour the grace of God out on people in your life who are undeserving of it. Do not let unforgiveness reside in your heart. Let the love of Christ dwell richly in your heart; forgive others, and watch God transform your life for the better.

Prayer: "Lord, I ask for Your strength to help me forgive. Give me the strength to extend grace to those in my life that have wronged me. Give me the strength to forgive my enemies. Give me the grace to restore relationships well that You desire for me to have. Lord, I don't want to feel burdened by the weight of unforgiveness. I do not want to feel shackled in the chains of bitterness. Give me a heart of forgiveness. Help me to grow in compassion and mercy to extend to others. I pray I will never stop forgiving those who hurt or offend me. I pray You will help me to let go and uproot any bitterness that could be in my life causing me to be stuck and stagnant in life. God, I surrender my feelings to You and pray You will give me Your perspective on every issue I face in my life. Let Your heart be my heart. In Jesus, amen."

Reflection:

- After reading today's devotional, what is one thing God is saying to you?

- What does Matthew 18:21–22 mean to you?

- Are you harboring unforgiveness in your heart? Is there anything you need to let go of or anyone you need to forgive?

- Write down any other thoughts you have.

- Meditate on Matthew 18:21–22 today.

DAY 19

God Is Good, All the Time

Taste and see that the Lord is good; blessed is the one who takes refuge in Him.

—Psalm 34:8 (New International Version)

One of my favorite songs is "You Keep on Getting Better," by Maverick City. The chorus is the section of the song I enjoy the most. In the chorus, the singers sing, "You are good," over and over. The first time I heard this song, I just could not get it out of my head. I would wake up singing it and would play it right before I would lie my head down on my pillow to sleep, meditating on the lyrics, "You are good."

Do you believe that God is good?

Sometimes we question the goodness of God when we get stuck in the past or dwell on the hurt and pain of life. Life sure does confront us with painful circumstances, but when we let our pain cause us to doubt God's unfailing love and care for our lives, we begin to lose sight of who God is.

We began to wonder: Can I rely on God? Does God care for me? Is He really good?

The answer is *yes*. God is always good, and we can always trust that He loves us and wants nothing but the best for our lives, even if it means experiencing troubles and difficulties to transform into the new creature God desires us to be. If we look at our pain and burdens of life instead of the good character of God, we begin to forget that God is higher than our difficulties. Whenever we face trials and storms of many kinds, we must look to and lean on the only One who can miraculously turn situations around for good. We must look to the only One who is able to carry all our burdens, while giving us His shoulder to rest on. Knowing God is knowing His goodness.

Knowing God is knowing His goodness.

Whenever we face trials and storms of many kinds, we must choose to shift our focus. Instead of focusing on the problems in front of us, we must choose to focus on the One who knows not only why these problems are occurring, but also how to get through problems. We must not focus on our lack but instead focus on the transforming power our God holds to bring about good from every bad situation we face. We must choose to focus on the healing we could be undergoing through our trials, the toxic thinking that is being uprooted, and the miracles and blessings we will eventually see when we come out of our trials.

Choose to narrow your focus on what truly matters—God getting His glory in our lives through every single good and bad thing we encounter!

God is not only good when things are going well. He is good when times seem troubling and out of control. He is good when our so-called friends betray us or a loved one passes away. When our finances go downhill, He is still good. When our jobs let us go, He is still good. God's goodness never fades away, even when our circumstances don't seem to be good at the moment. In our disappointments and hurts, we must choose to see God's goodness, even if it feels hidden like the sun behind the clouds on a dull day.

God is always with you, and He is always good, on the good days and not-so-good days.

As we draw closer to God amid our trials, we will begin to know and understand Him more clearly. We will begin to hear Him as He speaks to us and reveals to us how we can boldly walk through the fires of our lives with all confidence and faith that He is the God of Shadrach, Meshach, and Abednego, who will be with us through every fire we go through and has a good plan for every fire we experience. The more we trust in His goodness, the more we will learn and know Him better. When difficulty arises, be confident that you are held in God's capable and caring hands because He loves you just that much.

Prayer: "Lord Jesus, Your name is most powerful. I call on You, Jesus, because there is no way higher, no one better, and no one as good as You. I want to experience Your joy, not some of the time but all of the time. God, help me to know Your heart. I want to experience and trust in Your goodness, not some of the time, but all of the time. Help me to trust in Your goodness, no matter what trial or difficult circumstance I face. Even when the bad days begin to cloud me from seeing Your goodness, help me to stay assured regardless of how I feel or what I see; You are still good. In Jesus, Amen."

Reflection:

- After reading today's devotional, what is one thing God is saying to you?

- What does Psalm 34:8 mean to you?

- How has God demonstrated His goodness to you in your life? Do you find it hard to see God's goodness during difficult times in your life?

- Write down any other thoughts you have.

- Meditate on Psalm 34:8 today.

Only What You Do for Christ Will Last

For what shall it profit a man, if he shall gain the whole world, and lose his own soul?

—Mark 8:36 (King James Version)

"Only what you do for Christ will last," is a quote my father would say all the time when I was growing up. I truly didn't understand this quote until I grew older. It became even more real when I read about the parable of the talents in the Bible. In this parable, a man gave away talents to his servants. The man gave five talents to his first servant, two talents to his second servant, and one talent to the last servant. Then he went away. When he returned, he inquired about the talents he had given these servants. The one who had received five talents doubled it to ten talents. The one who had been given two talents made two more talents. But the last servant dug a hole into the ground and hid the only talent his master had given him. The man was pleased with the first two servants for how they had invested the talents he had given them but scolded the third servant for how he had not invested the one talent he had given him. Because of this lazy deed, the master took the one talent from him and gave it to the one who increased his talents to ten. This parable presents us with the topic of stewardship. A steward not only protects but expands the assets given to him or her. In this parable, a man entrusted three men to be good stewards of his possessions.

This, my friend, is an actual representation of what Jesus Christ does for us. If we are born-again believers, God has given us things to steward, and until our time ends or until He returns, we have talents (time, skills, gifts, abilities, and financial resources) to use for his kingdom purposes. One day, you must stand before God and give an account for your life. Did you use what you had been given so that you could make an eternal difference for God? Did you sacrifice your time, skills, spiritual gifts, abilities, and financial resources for Him? When you sacrifice for the Lord and His kingdom, He will always remember it. When you make Him first in your time, talents, and treasure, He will always remember it.

When you make Him first in your time, talents, and treasure, He will always remember it.

What skill have you been given? What gifts do you have? How much time and money do you invest in the work of God's kingdom? Like these servants in the parable, no two people on earth have the same abilities, gifts, time, and financial resources. Everyone is different, and God has blessed each person differently. God has given us all we have to develop so that we can use them to our best ability and for His great glory.

The question is what are you going to do with all that has been given to you? What you do for Christ will always last. Not only will you receive rewards here on earth, but you are building up treasures and rewards for yourself in heaven. What you sacrifice for the Lord, He will return with more than you could have ever imagined. Submit your life to God every day. Submit your time to God. Submit your gifts and abilities to God.

Submit your money and financial resources to God and watch Him transform your life.

> *Prayer: "Lord, help me to work as unto Christ and never cease to forget that only what I do for You will last. Lord, help me to live in light of eternity. Reveal to me the talent You have given me. Give me wisdom on how to be a good steward of my possessions. Give me knowledge and insight on how to use my talents, time, skills, gifts, and abilities for Your kingdom. My life belongs to you. Lord, reveal the skills and gifts You have given me for Your glory. Help me to embrace my uniqueness and who You have made me to be and not stray from the path You have called me to walk in. I trust You, Lord, amen."*

Reflection:

- After reading today's devotional, what is one thing God is saying to you?

- What does Mark 8:36 mean to you?

- What does the phrase "only what you do for Christ will last," mean to you?

- Write down any other thoughts you have.

- Meditate on Mark 8:36 today.

DAY 21

My God, My Exfoliator

And have put on the new self, which is being renewed in knowledge in the image of its Creator.

—Colossians 3:10 (New International Version)

I remember experiencing a really bad breakout after using a certain skin-care brand I had been using for almost two years. Suddenly one day, it just stopped working. Not only did it stop doing its job, but it completely turned on me and broke out my skin badly. It got so bad that I prayed to God one night and asked Him to show me a new skin-care regimen. I lay down, and shortly afterward, God allowed an image to appear in my mind—a product I used to use when I was younger. This product was an exfoliating facial peel. I purchased it that night, and I saw amazing results after using it for just a few days.

Our skin naturally sheds dead skin cells to make room for new cells often. Sometimes, the dead cells don't shed off completely and can result in dry skin, flaky patches, and clogged-up pores. Exfoliating can help prevent this.

Exfoliating is the process of removing dead skin cells from the outer layer of the skin's surface to improve the appearance of your skin. Exfoliate means to shed off in scales or layers.

Just as an exfoliator removes dead skin cells, spiritually we need God to be our exfoliator and remove dead patterns, thinking, and old ways in which we used to engage. We need to ask God to remove things not good for us—our old lifestyle and toxic behaviors so that we can be turned into something *new*! Our old, sinful lifestyles and impure ways of thinking may have worked for us for some years, but eventually we'll see the drastic results of sin. Colossians 3 is one of my favorite passages that come to mind when I think of God exfoliating us to make us new. This passage tells us to put to death whatever belongs to our earthly nature such as sexual immorality, impurity, and evil desires; it tells us to rid ourselves of things such as slander, rage, anger, malice, and filthy language. This passage further explains how we should refrain from lying. Instead, it encourages us to display compassion, kindness, gentleness, patience, humility, love, and forgiveness.

We must daily ask the Lord to remove what is not like Him and replace it with what is like Him. We must ask Him to remove relationships, environments, toxic patterns, and ways that are not like Him and replace it with what will help us become more like Him. Letting go of our old ways is necessary for us to become new in Christ. And spending time with God in His Word, worshiping

> *We must daily ask the Lord to remove what is not like Him and replace it with what is like Him.*

Him, praying, fasting, and spending time with other believers are some of the things we must do so we can transform into the new being God desires us to be. Do you want to become all that God desires for you to be? If you do, allow God to exfoliate you every single day.

Prayer: "Lord, I believe You are a God of new beginnings. I believe You are a God who takes old and makes it new. I believe in the promises You have already given me in Your Word, that You will never leave or forsake me, that You are in control, that You are good, and that You have forgiven me of my sins. Lord, be my exfoliator. Remove what is not like You and replace it with what is like You. Lord, I always rejoice because You are always performing miracles and transforming the lives of those who place their trust in You. I pray that You speak to me and show me how I should go so I can continue to experience the transformation You are doing in my life to mold me from old to new. Guide me so that I walk on the path You have set for me and experience all You have in store for me. Hold my hand as I live out the destiny You have given me."

Reflection:

- After reading today's devotional, what is one thing God is saying to you?

- What does Colossians 3:10 mean to you?

- Do you sense God removing things not of Him in your life? Do you sense Him adding beneficial people and things to your life? What are some things you can do to become all that God desires for you to be?

- Write down any other thoughts you have.

- Meditate on Colossians 3:10 today.

DAY 22

Faith That Heals

And a woman was there who had been subject to bleeding for twelve years. She had suffered a great deal under the care of many doctors and had spent all she had, yet instead of getting better, she grew worse. When she heard about Jesus, she came up behind him in the crowd and touched his cloak, because she thought, "If I just touch his clothes, I will be healed." Immediately her bleeding stopped, and she felt in her body that she was freed from her suffering. At once Jesus realized that power had gone out from him. He turned around in the crowd and asked, "Who touched my clothes?" "You see the people crowding against you," his disciples answered, "and yet you can ask, 'Who touched me?'" But Jesus kept looking around to see who had done it. Then the woman, knowing what had happened to her, came and fell at his feet and, trembling with fear, told him the whole truth. He said to her, "Daughter, your faith has healed you. Go in peace and be freed from your suffering."

—Mark 5:25–34 (New International Version)

In my senior year of high school, I began experiencing issues with my health. It started with just headaches at random moments of the day, but then my health progressively got worse to the point I would visit one doctor to the next trying to discover the root cause of my pain. As the years progressed, I began to lose so much weight unintentionally. One day, I was in so much pain that my father had to rush me to the hospital for doctors to give me medication to lessen the pain. One year, I spent thousands of dollars on a four-month health program that guaranteed I would improve once I finished the program, but it did not fulfill its promise. Doctors would tell me all kinds of things that were going on, but no doctor could ever give me a solution. Finally, I gave up and began to seek the Lord about supernatural healing.

In October 2021, as I fasted and prayed for healing, I decided to listen to the audio version of the Bible on YouTube. I was listening to an audio version as I slept hard one night, and I randomly woke up in the middle of the night to Mark 5:27–29. In this passage, I was reminded about the woman with a blood issue for twelve years who only touched the hem of Jesus's garment for her healing. I immediately knew that this was not random and that the Lord had allowed me to wake up to this passage. I knew it was a divine moment to remind me that God is my Healer and to demonstrate faith in His power to heal.

Maybe right now, you are experiencing sickness, pain, past trauma, or a broken heart that you are asking for God to heal. The Lord knows what you are struggling with. And He knows exactly what you need. God promises He will never leave or forsake you. He is your provision, and there is a healing power that you have access to through Jesus Christ. All you need to do is have faith.

Don't worry about the outcome; God is in control. Believe for it and have faith in God that He is going to use everything that you are going through for His good.

All you need to do is have faith.

The beautiful thing about the woman who entered Jesus's presence and was healed from her blood issue of twelve years is that Jesus not only healed her, but He enabled her to experience a true relationship with Him. Before he healed her, she just knew Him as a man who could heal, but after he healed her, she now knew Him as *"her healer."* My friend, you may be longing for healing and comfort from Jesus, but when you enter His holy, powerful presence, you get so much more! Jesus is not only your Healer; He is your Provider; He is your Savior; He is your Protector, and He is your Comforter. Jesus wants to do more than just heal our wounds and answer our prayers. He wants us to experience a true, deep, loving relationship with Him. Enter God's presence, not just for your healing but because you desire to draw closer to Him. Get into God's presence so that He can speak to you, show you truths about Himself and give you the faith you need to be healed. After He heals you, share this testimony with others to encourage them to believe that what God did for you, He can do for them! Let God be glorified publicly in your healing. Your healing story will be a testimony for all who hear.

Prayer: "Lord, I believe You are my healer. Lord, I pray that You touch every single area I seek healing. Lord, You know my thoughts and my desires. You are my Provider and can take care of my needs. I pray You provide for my needs and bless me with so much more than I could have ever imagined. Lord, I pray for strength, good health, and Your power to press through this day with gratitude. Thank You for Your supernatural healing to bring restoration to any part of my life that needs Your supernatural power. I believe You are my Provider and can heal any area of my life that is broken emotionally, spiritually, physically, or mentally. I pray that You strengthen my faith so that my faith can heal me just like the woman with the blood issue of twelve years. She trusted You and demonstrated her faith by touching the hem of Your garment, and with one touch she was granted access to Your healing power. Lord, I have faith in Your power to heal me. You alone are my Healer. Grant me a testimony to share with others for Your glory. In Jesus's name, amen."

Reflection:

- After reading today's devotional, what is one thing God is saying to you?

- What does Mark 5:25–34 mean to you?

- In what ways are you seeking healing? Do you trust in God's power to heal you just as He did for the woman with the blood issue of twelve years, or are you struggling with unbelief?

- Write down any other thoughts you have.

- Meditate on Mark 5:25–34 today.

DAY 23

Enduring Trials, Temptations, and the Wilderness

Consider it pure joy, my brothers and sisters, whenever you face trials of many kinds, because you know that the testing of your faith produces perseverance. Let perseverance finish its work so that you may be mature and complete, not lacking anything.

—James 1:2–4 (New International Version)

In 2017, I had a dream of me trapped in a room with no help or support. Every corner that provided a way of escape was blocked by enemies, which prevented me from getting out. Immediately I heard, "Jump; everything will work out; safety is in my hands." I looked up and noticed there was an open window in front of me. At that moment, I took a leap of faith, jumped out the window, and walked on the air down to the ground, landing safely. There were other people trapped in the room who, after seeing me jump, followed my example, and were also brought to safety. This dream left me with assurance that in the face of danger, God will always make a way out. Moreover, my leap of faith that I take in any situation will always inspire others to follow my example and take a leap of faith for themselves.

Trials, temptations, and dark moments are for a reason—to train and develop you into the person God has called you to be. Training by God develops humility, character, and obedience. The wilderness reveals to you that God is, sure enough, your provider because He "makes a way in the wilderness and streams in the wasteland" (Isaiah 43:19, New International Version). Your story does not end with your current trial. God will always make a way out for you if you trust Him. He is Jehovah Jireh, our Provider. If God ever calls you into the wilderness, know that He will also call you through it. There is always purpose in the wilderness. There is always something new God does in the wilderness. The wilderness is for transformation. The wilderness is for growth. Don't be like the Israelites and prolong your time in the wilderness by complaining. Pray and fast in the wilderness, and let God teach you that He is your source. You are in training, and when you pass this training, you will become all that God wants you to be.

Trials, temptations, and dark moments are for a reason—to train and develop you into the person God has called you to be.

In your wilderness season, God wants to detox, purge, disciple, direct, and heal you. God wants to mature you spiritually. You are His student. He is your professor. Follow His syllabus. You are a soldier. He is your commanding officer. Follow His order. With obedience comes wealth, blessings, evolutions, and transformed souls that are led to Christ through your godly example. In the wilderness, God will break you to make you, but in doing so, He will teach you principles and give you wisdom and knowledge so that you know how to act when you get out.

When life gets hard, lean on God to get you through. Speak life over your life and words consistent with the promises of God in His Word. Don't get chained to words of self-defeat and your limitations. Don't lose hope in the wilderness and doubt you will ever get out. Instead, trust God's timing, and get as much as you can in this training season, in this wilderness. Persevere, trust God, and obey so you can make it to the promised land. Don't give up if you are in your wilderness season. Endure through your trials. Press through the wilderness knowing that God has bigger plans than you can ever imagine, but He can't put you on the next level without you passing the tests on your current level. Your weeks, months, and years of training will all be worth it. Your big moment is coming.

Prayer: "Lord, help me to fight. Lord, encourage me to believe that I am not fighting for victory, but that I am fighting from a place of victory I have already won through Jesus Christ! Help me to persevere through life trials with contentment and joy, knowing that the testing will allow me to become all that You desire for me to be. Make a way out for me when I face temptation, and help me to endure each trial that comes my way. I pray I am stronger, better, and wiser each time I overcome a battle. Allow me to sense Your comfort, provision, and protection in the wilderness. You are Jehovah Jireh, my Provider. I pray for Your supernatural power to help me persevere through life's difficult moments. Help me to take a leap of faith so that I can inspire others to take leaps of faith. Make a way out for me in the wilderness. Purge, detox, and heal me in the desert. Help me to pass this training and obey Your every command to overcome. And when I overcome, allow the words of my testimony to help win other souls to Christ. I trust You, God. In Jesus's name, amen."

Reflection:

- After reading today's devotional, what is one thing God is saying to you?

- What does James 1:2–4 mean to you?

- What trials are you enduring in this season? What are some things you can do to help you persevere through these trials?

- Write down any other thoughts you have.

- Meditate on James 1:2–4 today.

DAY 24

Prayerlessness

Confess your faults one to another, and pray one for another, that you may be healed. The effectual fervent prayer of a righteous man availeth much.

—James 5:16 (King James Version)

Prayerlessness comes with a price. Neglecting prayer can result in discouragement, weariness, and delays. Our Father never ceases to invite us to come to Him with all our concerns, petitions, gratitude, and requests, so why not come to Him? Why wait until our situations take a spiritual, emotional, or even physical toll on us? God never made us carry our burdens alone, but He commands us in 1 Peter 5:7 (New International Version) to cast our "anxiety on Him because He cares" for us. God wants to carry us through every trial, every test, and every trying situation. He is strength in our weakness. He is the solution to our problems.

No weight is too heavy for God to handle. There is no giant too big for God to defeat. When we allow God to carry our burdens, our troubling situations will feel so much lighter. Let prayer be a priority in your life, and trust God to see you through. Spend alone time with God every day for Him to speak to you and show you how to carry your day and whatever task that comes along with it. Even

Jesus slipped away sometimes to pray to God, alone. Even Jesus knew how important it is to avoid seeking man-made options and instead seek God's opinion. When we seek God's face through prayer and let Him take full control of our situations, we begin to see Him move! We begin to see him change us from the inside out. We begin to feel His strength that supports us in our every weakness. And this act of surrendering delights God.

Do not wait until you are in an emergency to call upon the Lord. Do not be a believer who does not bother talking to the Lord until he or she feels that problems are too heavy to carry. Go to God now, in every season of your life, both good and bad, with gratitude for what He's done thus far and faith in His power to continue to do His great work! Avoid seeking counterfeit options as solutions to your earthly problems. Counterfeit options, such as idols that try to take the place of God in your life, last only for a little while, and some can even lead us away from God's plan and will for our lives. They cause us more pain and destruction and, in the end, bring about negative consequences.

And this act of surrendering delights God.

Instead of seeking these counterfeit options, seek God in prayer. If you sense any conviction you need to spend more time with the Father, confess prayerlessness in your life and ask God to give you the strength, patience, and desire to spend more time with Him each day.

As you pray the prayer, picture Jesus beside you taking the burdens you've placed on your shoulder onto His. "Praise be to the Lord, to God our Savior, who daily bears our burdens" (Psalm 68:19, New International Version).

Prayer: "Lord, thank You that I can come boldly to Your throne of grace at any moment of my life. Thank You for always hearing my prayers. Lord, I pray that You give me supernatural strength to pray without ceasing. Help me to come to You about every question or concern I have in every area of my life. Help me to obey Your voice when You answer my prayers by telling me yes, no, or just wait. Reveal to me how to overcome each trial and temptation I face. I want to see Your kingdom come and Your will be done. In Jesus's name, amen."

Reflection:

- After reading today's devotional, what is one thing God is saying to you?

- What does James 5:16 mean to you?

- What are some things you are praying for? How has God been faithful to your prayers in the past?

- Write down any other thoughts you have.

- Meditate on James 5:16 today.

The Power of Wisdom and Community

If any of you lacks wisdom, you should ask God, who gives generously to all without finding fault, and it will be given to you.

—James 1:5 (New International Version)

The Lord God said, "It is not good for the man to be alone. I will make a helper suitable for him."

—Genesis 2:18 (New International Version)

Two things that come to my mind when I think of ways believers can grow spiritually are wisdom and community. We must never fail to seek wisdom and community in our faith journey with the Lord.

Wisdom comes with a great price, but though it costs, we must get it at all costs.

Wisdom is one of the most important things we must get in our walk with Christ. Wisdom comes with a great price, but though it costs, we must get it at all costs. Wisdom will not only protect you, but it will enable you to stand out in the crowd and use your voice to leave people speechless. It will allow you to speak words that none of your adversaries or enemies can contradict.

Wisdom is far better than the treasure and knowledge the world tries to offer. Nothing can compare with wisdom from God. And so at all costs, we must seek wisdom. We must never fail to ask God to give us wisdom to help us in our everyday lives to not only navigate through life's trials but to help us to know what or what not to say in the face of our adversaries.

Another thing we should get on our faith journey is community. Community is something we need to spiritually grow into the person God wants us to be. God did not make us to be alone. In fact, in Genesis, God reveals to us that it is not good for man to be alone. To accomplish God's agenda, we need the body of Christ. To carry out the gospel, we need the church. To make it through life's trials, we need our fellow brothers and sisters in Christ. We aren't just here for ourselves; we are here to glorify God and to advance His kingdom. We are here to be built up and help build up our fellow brothers and sisters in Christ. We cannot be solo Christians. We must aim to function together because each of our individual parts is critical to the body of Christ. Individually, it is important for us to divinely use the God-given gifts, talents, abilities, skills, and resources God has given us to advance His kingdom.

We cannot be solo Christians.

I encourage you to never fail to seek wisdom. I encourage you to never fail to seek community. Ask God for wisdom that leaves people speechless. Ask God to nourish your relationships with other believers. If you are lacking a community, ask God to send you brothers and sisters in Christ who can assist you on your walk with the Lord. God will give us what we need. All we must do is ask.

Prayer: "Lord, thank You that I can come to You and ask for wisdom that You can generously give me. I pray that You increase Your wisdom and knowledge in my life so that I can live according to Your will and way You have set before me. Thank You that You have made community for me. Lord, I pray that You usher in the right people You desire for my life and strengthen the relationships and community You have already given me. Thank You for all that You have equipped me with for this journey to glorify You and help build Your kingdom. Continue to use me as You see fit. In Jesus's name, amen."

Reflection:

- After reading today's devotional, what is one thing God is saying to you?

- What do James 1:5 and Genesis 2:18 mean to you?

- List some areas of your life you need wisdom. List some people in your community.

- Write down any other thoughts you have.

- Meditate on James 1:5 and Genesis 2:18.

DAY 26

Be Faithful

He that is faithful in that which is least is faithful also in much: and he that is unjust in the least is unjust also in much.

—Luke 16:10 (King James Version)

Your gift will make room for you. In fact, "a man's gift maketh room for him, and bringeth him before great men" (Proverbs 18:16, King James Version). As believers, it is so important for us to be faithful in what God has called us to before God can promote us to the presence of great men. If we are faithful in the little things, God will bless us with much. If we are faithful over the few, we will naturally be faithful over many. Our commitment to the little will eventually allow God to bless us with more.

So right now, what is it that you have? Do what you can with the time, talents, gifts, and resources available to you right now. God will bless you with more in due time but be faithful to what lies in front of you now so that God can trust you with more later. If you desire more influence, more authority, more money, more friends, or even more land, be faithful to what God has given you right now. Steward over the blessings God has graced you to have right now. Every resource and every gift God has given you is an opportunity for you to serve God and others, and in doing so, God can multiply what you already have.

The story of the five loaves and two fish provides us with an example of how God can take our little and multiply it for the sake of not just blessing us but for also blessing other people around us. In this story, a great multitude that Jesus was teaching was hungry but had no food. The only food they found was two fish and five loaves of bread that a young boy had. In faith, the little boy gave everything he had to Jesus, which didn't seem like a lot, but because of Jesus's great power, He took that little and turned it into a lot to feed every single person in the crowd. There were even leftovers! Jesus can take our little and use it in such a way that it can bless us and others beyond our wildest dreams. He can take our little we do not think is much to offer and enable it to provide for generations and generations to come.

Jesus can take our little and use it in such a way that it can bless us and others beyond our wildest dreams.

Give your little to God. Use your talents for God when it seems as if no one is paying attention to you. Share your resources and money with others even when you feel that you do not have enough to give. Bring what you have to God and allow Him to raise you up to do more for His glory as you stay faithful with the little.

Prayer: "Lord, thank You for what You have given me. Thank You for entrusting me with all the blessings and gifts You have graced me to have. I ask that You help me to be faithful to all I have now and trust You to multiply what I already have for Your kingdom. Help me to wait on You as You work behind the scenes of my life and prepare me for the great things to come. Increase my gratitude and contentment with what I have now so that I am used to the greatest capacity in this season. Allow my gifts to make room for me and usher me into the presence of great men. In Jesus's name, amen."

Reflection:

- After reading today's devotional, what is one thing God is saying to you?

- What does Luke 16:10 mean to you?

- What are some things you are faithful to now? Do you sense that God is calling you to be faithful to anything else? What are some ways you can show God you are faithful to what He has given you now?

- Write down any other thoughts you have.

- Meditate on Luke 16:10 today.

DAY 27

Well Done, My Good And Faithful Servant

Whatever you do, work at it with all your heart, as working for the Lord, not for human masters, since you know that you will receive an inheritance from the Lord as a reward. It is the Lord Christ you are serving.

—Colossians 3:23–24 (New International Version)

How you live your life on earth determines how you live life in heaven. Luke 19 is one of my favorite parables that talks about the coming kingdom of God on earth. In this parable, Jesus tells a story of a man who had to go away to a distant country. In this parable, the man gives three of His servants one mina each to put the money to work, until he comes back. When he returns, he calls for the servants to account for the money and determine if they had stewarded it well. The first reports a profit of ten minas from the one mina given to him, which is a 1,000 percent increase; and the second a profit of five minas from the one mina. Because of this, the master rewards each with more responsibility due to the profit they made. But the third servant repays only the original mina, saying he only stored it away. The disappointed master punishes him by taking away the mina and rebuking him for not making use of it.

This story gives us a glimpse of what is to come in regard to how we will be rewarded in heaven. Basically, how did we use what God gave us in light of eternity? One day everyone will have to face the Judge, our Lord God. We will stand before God to be evaluated for who we are and what we have done. The purpose is to recompense us for what we have done, whether worthless or good; the good deeds will be rewarded, but the worthless will not. Believers won't be condemned on the day of judgment but will stand before Christ to give an account for their lives. His purpose is not to punish us but to evaluate and reward our good works.

In eternity, when we get to heaven as believers, we will not just be worshiping our Lord God, dancing and singing on clouds. The Bible tells us in Revelation 21:1 (New International Version) "a new heaven and a new earth" will be created and we will have great kingdom work to do in this new heaven and earth. There will be nations functioning, job responsibilities, assignments for believers, and things written about in Revelation 2:26–28, 20:4–6. Just like good employees get promotions, Christ's faithful followers will get promoted in eternity. But God will take away from believers that were not faithful with what they were given.

So, if you know Jesus now, live for Jesus now. Why get saved at twenty then wait another ten years to actually live for Jesus and get going for the Lord? Don't be a lukewarm, in-and-out Christian. Choose one Master. If you want to receive the best, give your best for the kingdom of God. Choose this day whom you will serve. Live for Christ so that you receive all that He wants you to receive on earth and in heaven. Use the gifts, talents, and skills that He has given you for His glory. Don't just

If you want to receive the best, give your best for the kingdom of God.

say you know Christ, let there be depth to your commitment to Christ; let there be fruit in your walk with the Lord.

And let God be your motivation for living for His kingdom. Yes, God is our Judge, but He is also our Savior. He loves us, died for us, and paid the penalty of sin for us, which is enough reason to motivate us to love Him and live for Him. He is our God that is for us, not against us, and delivered us from the penalty of death. You may be hidden now in the work that you do or in your hometown, but if you do what God has called you to do faithfully and consistently, you will be honored before all of heaven on the day we all must give an account. We are on this earth for God's glory. I know just like me, you want to hear, "Well done, my good and faithful servant," so live for the Lord.

Prayer: "Lord, thank You for giving me life. Thank You for the breath You have given me to live another day and fulfill the purpose You called me to. Help me to use every single gift, talent, ability, and skill You have so graced me to have for Your glory. Reveal the work You want me to do so that I continue to honor You. I desire to see the fruits of my labor and desire Your will to be done in my life. Help me to live life here on earth in such a way that people are changed and transformed through my witness for Christ. Help me not to waste time doing frivolous activities or indulging in laziness. I desire to receive all that You want me to receive on heaven and earth. Help me endure to live my life for Your glory, even in the hard moments of life until one day I hear You say, "Well done, my good and faithful servant. In Jesus's name, amen."

Reflection:

- After reading today's devotional, what is one thing God is saying to you?

- What does Colossians 3:23–24 mean to you?

- Are you using your gifts, talents, skills, and all that God has given you for His glory? What are some actions you can take today to ensure you are making the most of your time here on earth to advance God's kingdom?

- Write down any other thoughts you have.

- Meditate on Colossians 3:23–24 today.

DAY 28

The Great Commission

Therefore go and make disciples of all nations, baptizing them in the name of the Father and of the Son and of the Holy Spirit, and teaching them to obey everything I have commanded you. And surely I am with you always, to the very end of the age.

—Matthew 28:19–20 (New International Version)

As followers in Christ, the most important aspect of our role is to help make other followers of Christ. One of the most important things that matter most to Jesus Christ is our work in making disciples. We must be soul-winning believers! The verses above, Matthew 28:19–20, prove this, and are some of the last words Jesus left with us after His resurrection and before He ascended back into heaven. What was at the forefront of God's mind? Making disciples of Christ.

We are to make other disciples of Christ and be disciples of Christ. To be a disciple, we must deny ourselves daily, take up the cross and follow Christ. Even when *To be a disciple, we must deny ourselves daily, take up the cross and follow Christ.* difficulties and trials come our way, we must not give up on this assignment to try to persevere through life. If we fail to do this, we will miss out on the great things God is doing in our lives. In fact, the Bible says, "For whoever wants to save their life will lose it, but whoever loses their life for me will find it" (Matthew 16:25, New International Version).

We are to spread the good news—Jesus's death, burial, and resurrection. In making disciples, we fulfill this command from God and greatly impact the world for Christ. Not only should we share the good news about Jesus Christ, but we should continue to encourage and invest in the new followers of Christ—our fellow brothers and sisters in Christ who are brought to the Lord through the work of the Great Commission, especially believers who may not know where to start when growing their relationship with God, or how to begin to pray and read the Bible.

As followers of Christ, we have an advantage when it comes to fulfilling our duty as followers of Christ. We have the Holy Spirit residing within us, and with the Holy Spirit, we have power and authority. With the Holy Spirit, we can share the good news with confidence that God has given us everything we need to help us fulfill this task in our neighborhood, at our workplace, at school, and anywhere and everywhere we go!

Choose today to commit yourself to be a disciple of Christ. Believe you have the power and authority from God to fulfill this task. Identify with Jesus Christ and ask Him to give you the wisdom and grace to share the good news! Ask the Holy Spirit to guide you and help you to carry out this mission. God will use you in ways you never thought possible as you help transform lives for His glory!

Prayer: "Lord, I accept Your call to be a disciple. I ask that You give me everything that I need to fulfill this assignment. Thank You for giving me the Holy Spirit to guide and lead me as I carry out this task. Give me the power and faith I need to successfully do what You have called me to do. I thank You for the transformation that is to come, in my life and in the lives of others I witness to. In Jesus's name I pray, amen."

Reflection:

- After reading today's devotional, what is one thing God is saying to you?

- What does Matthew 28:19–20 mean to you?

- Have you committed your life to be a full-time disciple? What are some ways you can go and make disciples?

- Write down any other thoughts you have.

- Meditate on Matthew 28:19–20 today.

DAY 29

The Advocate, The Holy Spirit

But the Advocate, the Holy Spirit, whom the Father will send in my name, will teach you all things and will remind you of everything I have said to you.

—John 14:26 (New International Version)

Do not get drunk on wine, which leads to debauchery. Instead, be filled with the Spirit, speaking to one another with psalms, hymns, and songs from the Spirit. Sing and make music from your heart to the Lord.

—Ephesians 5:18–19 (New International Version)

God will always equip us to do His will. He will give us everything we need so we can courageously move forward with confidence for each new endeavor. One of the ways God equips us is by giving us the Holy Spirit. The Holy Spirit gives us the power to accomplish every assignment God gives us. The power of the Holy Spirit will always be greater than any task in front of us. The Holy Spirit is our helper and our advantage that supplies us with truth, wisdom, intellect, and guidance, as we journey through the assignment, task, and calling God has given each of us.

The Holy Spirit isn't optional. Our relationship with the Holy Spirit is extremely important. As followers of Christ, we cannot successfully accomplish anything God has called us to without the power of the Holy Spirit. We must be full of the Holy Spirit, and one way we can do this is by placing ourselves in environments that are filled with Him. The Holy Spirit can be felt when you are sitting in service surrounded by other believers listening to your pastor preach or when you are by yourself, listening to worship music or praying. The Holy Spirit can even be felt as you experience conviction after sinning.

The Holy Spirit is our guide that enables us to receive exact instructions for the specific will God has for us. We not only receive guidance from the Holy Spirit; He also gives us ministry, manifestation, and motivational gifts. The ministry gifts enable us to be apostles, prophets, evangelists, pastors, and teachers. The Holy Spirit also gives motivational gifts that give us supernatural power in areas such as serving, encouraging, teaching, prophesying, giving, leading, and showing mercy. Lastly, the manifestation gifts of the Holy Spirit enable us to share wisdom, share knowledge, heal, demonstrate extraordinary confidence through the gift of faith, perform miracles, prophesy, discern between spirits, speak in tongues, and interpret tongues. With these gifts, we can fulfill the purpose and plans God has for our lives.

The Holy Spirit is our guide that enables us to receive exact instructions for the specific will God has for us.

If you know your gift, do your part, and build God's kingdom! If you are unsure, seek God's face and ask Him to reveal what it is

He has called you to and the gifts He has given you to fulfill your calling.

Jesus did His part through His life on earth and His death and resurrection, and He has left the Holy Spirit for us to do our parts!

Prayer: "Lord, thank You for Your Holy Spirit. Thank You for the guidance, wisdom, and direction I have through Your Spirit. Thank You for equipping me with everything I need to fulfill Your will. I pray that every day I am fueled with Your power as I seek Your face. I pray that I grow deeper in You as I journey through life, dependent on the Holy Spirit's voice for discernment and direction. Never cease to show me Your will, piece by piece, step by step. In Jesus's name I pray, amen."

Reflection:

- After reading today's devotional, what is one thing God is saying to you?

- What does John 14:26 and Ephesians 5:18–19 mean to you?

- Do you sense the Holy Spirit active in your life? What are some ways you activate the Holy Spirit in your life?

- Write down any other thoughts you have.

- Meditate on John 14:26 and Ephesians 5:18–19 today.

DAY 30

"Put It Back"

For God hath not given us the spirit of fear; but of power, and of love, and of a sound mind.

—2 Timothy 1:7 (King James Version)

Finally, brothers and sisters, whatever is true, whatever is noble, whatever is right, whatever is pure, whatever is lovely, whatever is admirable—if anything is excellent or praiseworthy—think about such things.

—Philippians 4:8 (New International Version)

For the first time in my life, I did twenty-one days of fasting and praying in 2019. On the day I began, I said to the Lord, "Lord show me *You*!" That same night, God began speaking to me through a dream. In my dream, I was taking things off a shelf that did not belong to me. As I was doing this, I immediately heard a voice in my dream say, "Faith, those thoughts you think are not mine, my thoughts are not your thoughts, says the Lord." When I woke up, I remembered the dream (sometimes I forget dreams, so this was miraculous) and began to think about what God could be saying to me. "Put it back," I thought to myself.

My friend, I want to encourage you to put it back. Put back the thoughts, the lies, the fears, and the doubts where they came from, the enemy. Put back whatever it is the enemy is trying to have you dwell on. The devil attacks your mind because he knows that if he has your mind, he can determine the outcome of your life because as a man thinks in his heart, so is he (Proverbs 23:7, New King James Version). God is not behind our thoughts of impurity. God is not behind our thoughts of lies. God is not behind our thoughts of fear. God has not given us a spirit of fear. God has given us a spirit "of power, and of love, and of a sound mind" (2 Timothy 1:7, King James Version). Tell yourself, "I have a sound mind." Repeat this until it sinks into your soul and permeates your mind. Ask God to heal and transform your mind. In and of ourselves, we do not have the power to transform our minds, but thankfully we serve a God who does. Let God

Tell yourself, "I have a sound mind."

transform your thought patterns. Let Him govern your mind. A mind governed by the Holy Spirit is a mind full of peace because God keeps those in perfect peace whose minds are focused on Him because they trust in Him (Isaiah 26:3, English Standard Version). When ill thoughts or thoughts of fear, doubt, or confusion arise, take "captive every thought to make it obedient to Christ" (2 Corinthians 10:5, New International Version). Demolish thoughts that are not of Christ. Dwell on thoughts that align with what God's Word says. Meditate on thoughts that resemble whatever is "true, whatever is noble, whatever is right, whatever is pure, whatever is lovely, whatever is admirable, excellent or praiseworthy" (Philippians 4:8, New International Version). Through meditating on thoughts that are pleasing to God (even if our reality and current circumstances are weighing us down), our minds can be conformed to resemble the mind of Christ.

Prayer: "Lord, I believe You are a mind transformer. Heal my mind, Lord. Transform my mind and help me to change my thoughts that are not pleasing in Your sight. Help me to not "conform to the pattern of this world," but instead be "transformed by the renewing of my mind" (Romans 12:2, New International Version). I commit my thoughts to You so that You can do a work in my mind and replace every single wrong and evil thought with Your truth and light. I trust in You to direct my thoughts so that my life can be directed in the way that You have planned for me to go. Do a work in my mind and reveal Your ways and thoughts to me. Give me thoughts that are consistent and in alignment with what You have already spoken to me in Your Word. In Jesus's name, amen."

Reflection:

- After reading today's devotional, what is one thing God is saying to you?

- What does 2 Timothy 1:7 mean to you? What does Philippians 4:8 mean to you?

- What is your thought life like? Do you struggle with negative and destructive thoughts? What are some ways you let God penetrate your mind with His truth so you can think thoughts pure, praiseworthy, and excellent?

- Write down any other thoughts you have.

- Meditate on 2 Timothy 1:7 and Philippians 4:8 today.

DAY 31

Ask and You Will Receive

Ask and it will be given to you; seek and you will find; knock and the door will be opened to you.

—Matthew 7:7 (New International Version)

I cannot believe we are at the end of this devotional. First, I want to applaud you. You've dedicated so much time drawing closer to God. I am so proud of you. I also want to thank you for taking this to deepen your relationship with God with these devotionals designed to encourage you in your faith walk. My prayer is that you continue to dive deep into the Word of God and daily pray to Him. And I pray you read this journey as many times as you need to help you grow stronger in your faith.

Regardless of where you are, physically or spiritually, know that the Lord has so much in store for you, my friend. Seek Him continuously. He wants to show you the plans He has for your life. He wants to reveal to you things unknown that will help you walk on the path and purpose He has specifically designed for you. He wants to give you everything He has stored up for you, but He's waiting on you. He's waiting on you to ask Him. Ask Him for whatever it is in your life you are seeking for Him to do. Cry out to Him repeatedly until you receive an answer from Him. Keep knocking on His door until it opens and until you discover the blessing God has in store for you. And it's not just one blessing, my friend. God wants you to experience an overflow of blessings. He wants you to have an overflow of peace, an overflow of joy, an overflow of hope, and so much more.

God's hand is never too short to provide for you and take care of your needs. God has not forgotten about you. He is always here with you and knows your thoughts and unspoken prayers. Trust Him in the unknown to provide answers for you.

Sometimes, we can get so overwhelmed and warped up by the difficult circumstances life presents that we lose sight of who God is. But today, I want to remind you that God is our deliverer and our Friend. He is the best solution giver to any issue we face in life. Never cease to call upon Him. God has unfailing love and care for you, and your faith can only be strengthened as you seek His face.

My hope is that this devotional opens your eyes to see the favor of God over your life. My prayer is that you will continue to call upon God. The more you do, the closer you will feel to Him, and there's no better feeling than experiencing God, His love, and all that He has in store for you.

Everything God has promised you is already yours, my friend. God is just waiting on you to ask.

Everything God has promised you is already yours, my friend. God is just waiting on you to ask.

Prayer: "Lord, I trust You. I trust You to meet my needs and give me understanding and guidance in the unknown when I cannot see which way to turn. You are near to me, even though sometimes I may feel alone. Lord, I know You know, see, and care for my every need. I pray that You give me the confidence to go boldly before Your throne of grace any and every time I need You, so that I can receive Your will for me. Give me the strength to never stop knocking on Your door. I believe in Your power to open the window of heaven for me so that I can receive a blessing so great I have no room to store and can only share with others. In Jesus, amen."

Reflection:

- After reading today's devotional, what is one thing God is saying to you?

- What does Matthew 7:7 mean to you?

- What is something you are asking God to do? Do you have faith He can do this for you?

- Write down any other thoughts you have.

- Meditate on Matthew 7:7 today.

Printed in the United States
by Baker & Taylor Publisher Services